The

Parrots And
Talking Birds

Manual

1

Alkeith O Jackson

The Parrots And Talking Birds Manual

Pet Owner's Guide To Keeping, Feeding, Care And Training

Alkeith O Jackson

Copyright Notice

Copyright, Legal Notice and Disclaimer

Contents

Preface: Talking Birds And Parrots

There are many species of parrots scattered over all parts of the world, and they vary in size from the diminutive paroquets to the great gaudy macaws and cockatoos. The parrots and their relatives are mostly brilliantly or strikingly colored birds, the prevailing hue of most species being green. The African Gray Parrot is the only gray species kept in captivity, while the various Australian Cockatoos are the only white ones.

The majority of the parrots seen in confinement are American; the cockatoos, cockatiels, and Lories are Australian; the paroquets are American, African, Indian, and Australian, while the macaws are all American.

Although they come from such widely separated localities, the habits, food, and nature of nearly all parrots are similar.

In a wild state they live in flocks and feed upon fruit, nuts, seeds, and leaves, while the Australian "Kea" Parrot has learned to devour sheep kidneys and has proved very troublesome. Some of the parrot family lives on the ground, others in low bushes, and others in grass, but the majority live in the topmost branches of tall forest trees.

While they can all fly swiftly and far, yet they spend most of their time climbing deliberately about among the branches, using their strong curved bills like an extra foot.

Although their colors are often very brilliant, yet in their native haunts parrots are not easily seen among the foliage, and have a habit of sitting motionless when one is looking for them. They are noisy, loud-voiced creatures, and when undisturbed keep up an incessant babel.

Most of the species build their nests in hollow trees or excavate holes for themselves. Parrots are very long-lived and may live for a hundred years or more, and most species are hardy. Most people consider parrots strictly tropical birds, and, as a matter of fact, the majority of the parrot family is natives of warm climates. Several species, however, dwell in high, mountainous regions, where it is very cold, and one of the most beautiful species—the Carolina Paroquet was formerly found throughout the southern and eastern United States as far north as Ohio.

Parrots have always been noted for their ability to talk, and in this respect there is a great difference between the species of parrots and even between individuals of one species. The question as to which kind of parrot is the best talker is one which will never be settled satisfactorily.

As a rule, the African Gray learns more readily than others, but the Panama green species, the various yellow-heads, and the Cubans all learn quickly.

Paroquets of some species learn to talk, and even macaws at times are splendid talkers. I have never seen a cockatoo that was really a good talker, but they are very intelligent and learn wonderful tricks.

I have recently seen a troop of trained cockatoos that were absolutely marvelous. One of these birds played "Home Sweet Home" by pulling strings attached to bells; another danced to music, and one rang any number which was called to it on a bell. This bird could add and subtract any number or combination up to twenty-five, and after looking at a watch or clock would ring the hour and minutes on a bell.

All the parrot family is intelligent and, if taken young and reared by hand will become gentle, docile, and affectionate. Many of the most beautiful species and the best talkers are seldom seen in captivity.

The great "Imperial Parrot" of Dominica Island, in the West Indies, learns to talk within a few weeks after taken from its native forests and even when captured fully grown he becomes perfectly gentle and affectionate within a week or two.

This splendid bird is wonderfully colored with royal purple, green, blue, and red, and is the largest of the true parrots.

Unfortunately, this bird has been so persistently hunted by the natives for food that the species has become rare, even in its native forests, and will probably be quite extinct before many years. Some of the Central American Paroquets are very beautiful and are well worthy of a place in our aviaries but are seldom seen in cages outside of their native land.

Introduction

Parrots Feeding and Care

The food now used generally for parrots over four months old consists of a mixture of equal parts of "paddy" or unshelled rice, hemp, and sunflower seeds. Cuttlefish bone should also be furnished, and a few peanuts may be given occasionally; other nuts should be avoided except cocoanuts. Parrots are very fond of these, and a small piece may be given once a week, but not oftener.

Parsley should be avoided as it poisons the birds, but lettuce, chickweed, and green or red pepper-pods are all excellent. A piece of raw onion is a good tonic, and apples, bananas, cherries, and other fruits will do no harm in reasonable quantities. Cracker, stale bread, and green corn (raw) are good for parrots, and if a piece of fresh sugar-cane or cornstalk can be obtained your pet will thoroughly enjoy it. Insects will be appreciated and are healthy, but sweetmeats, candy, cake, and meat are all objectionable.

Parrots require water, but sometimes a gray parrot cannot drink it without suffering from diarrhea, and in such cases clear black coffee should be given.

Plenty of gravel should be provided, for parrots love sand or gravel baths, and eat a great deal of gravel besides. The cage should be kept very clean and should be scrubbed with soap and water at least twice a week.

Few parrots will take water baths, but many paroquets will, and until you try you cannot tell whether your pets will bathe in water or not. Use a pint or a quart of tepid water, according to the size of the bird, and dissolve a spoonful of borax in it. If the birds will not bathe use an atomizer and spray them thoroughly two or three times a week.

Parrots may be kept either in cages or on stands, but as a rule the talking birds are kept caged and the cockatoos or macaws kept on stands. This method is almost a necessity

12

with the macaws, for their long tails are invariably worn or broken when in cages. Moreover, their powerful bills necessitate very strong cages, and they do fully as well if not better on the stands, where their beautiful colors and long tails show to best advantage.

Chapter 1

Training your Parrot to Speak

The whole secret in training parrots or other birds to speak, sing, or imitate any other sound is patience. We do not expect a child to learn to speak until several months old, and yet we often become discouraged and disgusted if a bird fails to learn to repeat a word, or -even a sentence, in the same length of time, or even less.

When teaching a parrot or other talking bird, let it remain for two weeks after it is purchased or acquired without other notice aside from feeding and caring for its wants. This will make it more at home and it will be less suspicious of your approaches. Then take away the drinking water or coffee for a few hours and offer it to the bird in your hand, at the same time holding out some favorite bit of food.

It will probably accept the drink and food from your hand and very soon will learn to perch on your hand or arm and will let you stroke or scratch its head.

Parrots learn to speak more rapidly if taught during the three or four hours after sunrise or before sunset, and the same word or sentence should be repeated over and over slowly, in clear, ringing tones, using care to always accent and pronounce the words in exactly the same way.

Never try to teach a bird to talk several different words or sentences at one time; wait until it has thoroughly mastered one thing before teaching another.

If the parrot pays no attention or fails to show any signs of learning its piece for several months do not despair. Sometimes a parrot may be taught for twelve months without its uttering a word, and then it will suddenly blurt out the complete sentence perfectly. After one or two simple things are learned the rest is an easy matter, and the bird will soon

15

learn to repeat long sentences, songs, etc. If you ever notice your parrot quietly muttering or talking in an undertone to itself do not interrupt or disturb it; it shows it is practicing its lesson, and if left alone it will perfect its pronunciation until sure of itself.

After speaking any word or sentence that has been taught, the bird should be rewarded by some tidbit. Rewards are far more efficacious than punishment when training parrots, and if allowed to grow really hungry and then fed when the words are spoken to it the bird will often learn more rapidly.

Chapter 2

Diseases Of Parrots

If parrots are correctly fed, are kept clean, and are cared for properly they will have few diseases and may live as long as or longer than their owners. The principal diseases and their remedies are given below, but in every case you must use judgment, and if in doubt consult some reliable bird-fancier, especially one that is accustomed to handling and keeping parrots.

Colds

Keep the bird in a warm place and give a few red peppers. Ten drops of aconite in a glass of water, to be given a teaspoonful at a time at intervals of an hour, is a good remedy. Clean the bird's nostrils with a feather dipped in salt water and moisten them with almond-oil.

Rub the throat and back with a solution of one part chlorate of kali in twenty parts of hot water. Let the bird inhale tar vapor from a bottle containing one part of tar to twenty-five parts of hot water.

Vomiting

This may be caused by fright, anxiety, overeating, or inflammation of the stomach. The former causes are of little account and the bird will soon recover; but if caused by inflammation and accompanied by weakness, shivering, loss of appetite, and bloody discharges, it should be promptly treated in the following manner:

Apply warm or nearly hot poultices of flaxseed to the stomach and belly and hold sand, as hot as you can bear in your hand, against the belly.

Give teaspoonful doses of a solution of tannin to seventy-five parts of water two or three times a day, and feed tea leaves that

18

have been steeped, and for a day or two mix tea with the drinking water.

Indigestion

Feed a plain, light diet of unshelled rice and a few hemp-seeds, without fruit or green food. Give some salt and tepid drinking water with a teaspoonful of lime-water in it. A teaspoonful of light Bordeaux wine may be poured down the parrot's throat.

Constipation

Use warm castor-oil and olive-oil in equal parts as an injection, using a small syringe for the purpose. Give a dose of ten drops of castor-oil with half a teaspoonful of honey once or twice a day, and feed hemp and sunflower seeds in equal parts, and a little fresh fruit and green food.

Diarrhea

Keep the parrot in a warm, quiet place, feed clear, unshelled rice, and give a cracker soaked in brandy and sprinkled with Cayenne pepper. If the attack is severe, put a few drops of paregoric in a teaspoonful of boiled milk and give this every three hours.

If the case is very severe and blood is passed give four drops of laudanum in the milk in place of paregoric and withhold all fruit, greens, and water until the bird recovers. Keep boiled milk with the laudanum and five to ten per cent of brandy in the cage.

Dysentery

Treat as for the last, and give in addition one half to one teaspoonful of castor-oil with ten drops of honey. Wash the fouled, sticky feathers under the tail with warm water and a few drops of oil of eucalyptus.

Pulling Feathers

This troublesome disease is due to improper food, such as meat, bones, too much sunflower seed, and lack of exercise. Feed only hemp and paddy, give abundant gravel and wood for the bird to gnaw, and furnish the bird with spools, small china toys, or metal rings to amuse him.

A half teaspoonful of glycerin in a teacup of tepid water used as a spray each day is excellent. Apple or banana should be fed daily. A salve or ointment especially prepared for the cure of this disease may also be used, and this is excellent.

All of the above directions as to food, care, and diseases apply equally well to the various parrots, paroquets, macaws, and cockatoos, and if in any case additional treatment or particular foods are required they will be mentioned under the description of the birds.

Chapter 3

The African Gray Parrot

This is the well-known "Joko" and is easily distinguished from all other parrots by its ash-gray plumage, whitish face, black bill, and red tail. For the first year the gray is quite dark and the tail is brown save close to the body, where a trace of red may usually be seen. The gray is a large bird in appearance, but the body itself is not as large as it seems, for the feathers are very thick. At times one may find a bird with a few red spots or feathers on the back, wings, or head.

Such birds are called "kings," and are supposed to be better than the ordinary birds and bring a higher price. This is pure imagination, for every species of known parrot is subject to variation in plumage, and no two individuals can be found which are absolutely alike in color.

Nearly every variety—especially those which normally have red in their plumage—is subject to great variation in the amount of red, and all are liable to have red feathers appear in odd or unusual places.

Such markings are purely individual variation, and the feathers frequently change their places with different molts. The presence of such "freaky" feathers has no bearing whatever upon the intelligence or talking ability of the bird.

Gray parrots are natives of central and western Africa and are brought to this country via England, South America, or direct in both steamships and sailing vessels.

Most of the gray parrots arrive in Boston, and those which arrive in sailing ships are the most prized, for having been longer on the trip they are more gradually accustomed to the change of climate, food, etc., and, moreover, are usually better cared for than those brought over on steamers.

Chapter 4

The Green Parrot

The commonest parrots are the various green varieties which are classed by bird dealers according to the localities from which they are brought. Some of these classifications are rather crude, and several distinct species are often found classed under one common name. Thus a "Panama" may be one of several related species, the "Yellow-Heads" belong to several species, and parrots of distinct kinds from Haiti, San Domingo, and Cuba are frequently all classed as "Cubans."

The leading green parrot is the Mexican or "Double Yellow-Head." This parrot is a beautiful clear green, with a pale-orange or deep-yellow forehead, white feet and bill, and blue and red feathers in wings and tail. It is larger than the gray parrot and is noted for its ability to learn songs. These parrots are also excellent talkers and whistlers.

Chapter 5

The Panama Parrots

The Panama is about the size of the Mexican, with an entirely green plumage except for a small yellow spot on the nape of the neck and the usual red and blue wing and tail feathers. Many people consider this bird a superior talker to the Mexican or the Gray Parrots.

The Carthagena

The Carthagena is named after the town of the same name in northern Colombia. It is a smaller bird than the Panama but is much like the Mexican in color, except that the beak is dark and the yellow forehead does not extend back over the crown in adult birds as does that of the Mexican Parrot.

The Amazon

The Amazon is a light-green bird with blue and yellow head, orange and red throat, scarlet-tipped wings, and parti-colored tail.

The Maracaibo

The Maracaibo is green with yellow forehead and variegated wings, and in general appearance is much like a small Mexican.

The Blue-Fronted Parrot

The Blue-Fronted Parrot is distinguished by its blue forehead, while the Cuban bird has a white forehead, scarlet throat, and red and blue wings.

Chapter 6

The Dwarf Parrots

Under this name we find several species of small parrots from South America, all of which are desirable cage-birds, very easily tamed and trained and most of them capable of learning to whistle and talk. They are very affectionate, and if kept in pairs they will show every sign of affection and devotion to each other.

They will eat together, share the same bath, and feed and preen each other. It is not necessary to keep them in pairs, for they live singly just as well, and their low price, intelligence, and ability to whistle or talk make them great favorites, especially with children.

As a pet the dwarf parrot, or "Beebee," is excellent; it becomes greatly attached to his master or mistress and is fond of being stroked or fondled. It loves to romp and play with the children and will play hide-and-seek with delight.

It is not destructive like the large parrots, and if allowed perfect freedom in a room will not get into any mischief. When kept in pairs and taught to speak the birds will often carry on a conversation in a most entertaining manner.

They should be kept in large cages and should be given a bath daily, for unlike most parrots they are fond of water. The best food for these birds is canary and hemp seeds in equal parts, with apple or other fruit daily.

If given a hollow limb or a box with a hole in one end they will breed and rear their young in confinement. The young birds up to six months old should be fed on soaked cracker.

This term is applied to various tiny parrots, some of which are gorgeously colored, and there are so many species that it is impossible to describe or mention them all. They are seldom capable of learning to talk, but many species whistle tunes, while others have a pleasing twittering song.

They are also capable of learning tricks, are readily tamed, they breed freely in captivity, and are very hardy. Their food should be canary-seed, with occasional hemp and sunflower, fresh apple, and greens.

They should be kept in pairs to thrive to best advantage, and are altogether very attractive and pleasing birds.

Chapter 7

The Grass Paroquet

The Grass Paroquet is a native of Australia, and is known by its pale yellowish-green color, yellow head, dark bars on the back, and blue spots on the throat and neck. This is the paroquet most commonly kept as a cage-bird and is the most easily cared for and hardiest species, although by no means the handsomest. They breed freely in captivity.

Love-Birds are tiny parrots which are much like the paroquets and dwarf parrots in habit. They are noted for their affection and attachment to their mates, and breed readily in confinement like paroquets.

Lories

These are gorgeously colored parrots from Australia. Their plumage is wonderfully variegated with red, blue, green, purple, orange, yellow, and other hues mingled in a perfect riot of color.

They are kept mainly for ornament, as they are not true talking birds and have harsh, unpleasant voices. Similar to the Lories are the lorikeets, which bear the same relation to the Lories that paroquets do to parrots.

Chapter 8

The Cockatoos

These are large, handsome birds from Australia. There are numerous species, the commonest being the Sulphur-Crested bird, with a beautiful curved crest of delicate sulphur yellow. The Rosy-Crested species has a salmon-pink crest, while the Lead-beater is delicately shaded with pink on the body, and has a deep salmon or fiery red and yellow crest.

Cockatoos sometimes learn to talk, but they may be taught many entertaining tricks and are suitable for ornamental birds, especially when kept on stands. Just as paroquets are diminutive parrots and lorikeets are miniature lories, so the large cockatoos are reproduced in pygmy size by the charming "cockatiels." These are beautiful birds of handsome colors, and should be kept by everyone fond of ornamental birds.

Chapter 9

The Macaws

There are three common species of these large, gorgeously colored American birds, known as the "Red Macaw," the "Blue Macaw," and the "Military or Green Macaw."

The red species is brilliant scarlet, with yellow, red, and blue wings and a long tail. The blue species is brilliant azure blue and bright yellow, while the Military Macaw is greenish with red and blue wings. They are easily kept but are better adapted to stands than cages. Occasionally they learn to talk splendidly, but as a rule they are merely kept as ornaments.

Their bills are extremely powerful and they are liable to inflict serious injuries if meddled with or handled. They are also likely to be treacherous and cannot be highly recommended as real pets.

The food may be the same as for parrots, but hard nuts, corn, and other hard grains may be fed, as such things keep the birds busy and prevent the bills from becoming overgrown.

Chapter 10

The Toucans

Of all odd and unusual birds these uncouth creatures stand at the head. Their enormous, brilliantly colored bills, gorgeous plumage, and odd voices make them attractive, and they are capable of becoming very tame and affectionate and may be taught to whistle, imitate various sounds, or even to talk.

Their natural notes sound almost human, and they are always lively, curious, interesting birds. They are most desirable pets, and whereas parrots are so common as to attract no interest or curiosity in the beholder, yet the toucans always attract attention and interest visitors.

When asleep these odd birds turn their huge bills over on their back and fold their tail, fan-like, over them, thus rolling themselves into a sort of ball.

There are various species, the commonest being the "Sulphur- Breasted," which is a black bird with sulphlir yellow and orange breast, pale green and red bill, and white eyes.

Other species have scarlet or white breasts; others are green with yellow throats; others are green and blue, green and red, black and orange, etc.

They may be kept in an ordinary cage or allowed considerable freedom when tame, and will thrive well on a varied diet of mocking-bird food, softened hemp and sunflower seed, fruit, greens, cooked rice or paddy, insects, and boiled potatoes.

They are very clean, tidy birds and love bright sunshine, and if properly fed and cared for will live many years in captivity.

Toucans are very fond of meat, and an occasional piece of fresh liver or a bit of fresh beef will not hurt them, while during the molting season hard-boiled egg may be given. Aside from this they should be treated much like parrots, as far as food, care, and diseases are concerned.

Chapter 11

The Crows

The common crow, ravens, European Crows, jackdaws, and others of the crow family are often kept as pets. If taken young and reared by hand they will become exceedingly tame and will learn to talk readily. The old idea that a crow's tongue must be slit to make him talk is ridiculous; the operation is as useless as it is cruel.

Kindness, care, and patience are the only means for teaching any bird to talk or imitate a sound, and as all the crow families are exceedingly intelligent they learn very readily.

Crows and their relations may be kept in cages, but it is best to give them as much freedom as possible. Feed them various seeds, fresh fruit, greens, plenty of insects, and a little egg in molting season and they will thrive and live for many years.

There is no bird that will thrive on a greater variety of diet and will be as free from diseases as the common crow, and none that will prove more amusing and entertaining.

This bird was called "Dom Pedro," after the emperor of Brazil, and was never kept confined in a cage except at night. He was full of odd tricks and kept us continually amused at his antics.

He learned to talk very soon, and would come when called like a well-trained dog. On one occasion he extracted all the goldfish from an aquarium, and the fish could not be found for months until one day when an old, unused dictionary was opened we found the unfortunates pressed between its pages.

On another occasion he robbed a pet rabbit of her babies and hid the poor creatures under the shingles of an outhouse roof. He was very fond of insects, and when my father was gardening Dom Pedro would follow about in his footsteps, and as soon as a worm or bug was turned up by spade or trowel he would rush forward and gobble it instantly.

A long story might be written to relate the numberless odd traits of this pet crow, but eventually his curiosity got him into trouble, and after eating a quantity of red paint he passed away, much to the sorrow of all who had known him.

Chapter 12

The Jays

Both the European Jay and the American Blue Jay make splendid pets, easily cared for, and capable of learning many tricks and to imitate the sounds of other birds and animals. Occasionally a jay may be taught to talk, and in my youth I owned a pet blue jay that spoke a number of words and several sentences. Feed the same as crows.

Magpies

Magpies are often kept as pets, and are very interesting and attractive. They are often taught to talk and will imitate various sounds and calls. They belong to the crow family and should be fed and cared for in the same way.

Chapter 13

The Motmots

These are very pretty and extremely curious birds, which are natives of tropical America. There are a number of species of motmots, but all are, more or less, alike in general appearance and in habits.

They are fairly large birds, about the size of jays, and are mainly blue and green in color, with very brilliant blue and black heads and long tails. The bill of the motmot is notched or toothed, and is very sharp and powerful.

In their native state these birds perch motionless upon a branch and dart into the air to seize passing insects, much as flycatchers do.

They also feed upon fish, frogs, and other water animals, which they catch after the manner of kingfishers, and they are fond of mice, small birds, lizards, and snakes. In captivity they will thrive on a mixed diet of meat scraps, insects, fruit, fish, and mocking-bird food.

Motmots are so tame, unsuspicious, and confiding that they are called "bobos," or "fools," by the natives, and when captured and caged they seem in no wise troubled or disconcerted at the change in their life.

These birds become exceedingly tame, they learn to answer to a call or whistle, and they will readily perch on one's finger or shoulder and feed from the hand.

They have no natural song and are rather silent birds, but are well worth keeping because of their docile natures and interesting habits. The most remarkable habit of the motmot is that he actually shaves.

The feathers of the tail, when they first grow out, are tapered and like any ordinary feather. For some reason the motmot thinks he can improve upon nature, and strips off the feathers on each side of the quill of the long tail-feathers, leaving the latter bare, except for a small tuft at the tip.

The Mynah

Parrots are world-famous as talking birds, and we usually consider them the best of talkers, but the East Indian "Mynah," or "Minor," is a far better conversationalist and a more entertaining pet.

It can learn an unlimited number of words and sentences can bark like a dog, meow like a cat, mimic odd sounds, or whistle tunes, and, best of all, it will invariably delight in showing off its attainments.

Many educated talking parrots are stubborn or bashful in the presence of strangers and utterly refuse to talk, sing, or whistle. The mynah, on the other hand, never has "stage fright" and will perform at command before a large audience.

These birds seem to know by intuition when callers have come to be entertained and will do all in their power to "show off" to the best advantage.

As an example of what a really well-taught mynah can do, I cannot do better than quote the words of Mr. Holden, who owns one of the most valuable of these birds. Mr. Holden says: "My own mynah talks and spells and laughs all day long, and every hour.

His cage is covered—except a 6-inch-wide space, the length of the top—at 6 p. m., but if uncovered during the evening he talks and laughs just as freely as during the day. He is wonderfully apt with his hearty laughter, followed by the remark: 'That's all right.'

When he thinks it is time to sleep, he says: 'Come and kiss me good night! Come and kiss nice!' Then he gives three long smacks and says: 'Ah, that's good!' On my return from a three months' trip I took him on my finger, where he likes to perch, and his prompt words, hitherto unheard by me, were:

'Three cheers for Holden!' It was a sweet welcome." Such a bird is valued at over one thousand dollars, but untrained mynahs may be purchased at from twelve dollars up.

The mynah is about the size of a small dove or a jay, with beak, feet, and legs orange-yellow. The plumage is mostly glossy, iridescent black, with reflections of violet,

51

green, and -bronze. The feathers, especially on the head, are very smooth and velvety, and below each eye is a small yellow naked "wattle," or membrane.

Behind the ears and extending beyond the back of the neck are other bright yellow, naked membranes or "ears," which may be raised or depressed by the bird. The only other markings are patches of snow-white on the wings.

It is an easily trained and affectionate bird and is very graceful in form and movements. All fruits, berries, and insects are suitable for the mynah, and it will readily eat prepared mocking-bird food with grated carrot and chopped hard-boiled egg.

It should bathe two or three times a week and should have a cage 20 to 24 inches in length, with gravel and cuttlefish bone. The mynah is a long-lived, healthy bird, and individuals have been known to live for seventy-five years or more.

The African Gray Parrot

Cockatoos

Cockatoos

Cockatoos

Macaws

Macaws

Macaws

Macaws

Alkeith O Jackson

Jays

Motmots

Motmots

Motmots

46885702R00037

Made in the USA
Columbia, SC
26 December 2018